Published 2010 by Concordia Publishing House
3558 S. Jefferson Avenue, St. Louis, MO 63118-3968
1-800-325-3040 • www.cph.org

Manufactured in China

2   3   4   5   6   7   8   9   10   19   18   17   16   15

When Someone Dies
Find Comfort in Jesus

By Julie Stiegemeyer
Illustrated by David Erickson

CONCORDIA PUBLISHING HOUSE · SAINT LOUIS

Have you ever lost a cherished toy or had to say good-bye to a close friend who moved away? At times like that, we feel sad.

But when someone we loved has died, we feel more than sadness. We also may be confused, scared, lonely, and maybe even angry. That jumble of feelings is called grief.

Grief means we feel sad and lonely and miss the person who has died.

"I miss Uncle Tommy. He made me laugh."
— Sasha, age 4

"I miss Grandma. I don't get to see her at family dinners."
— Riley, age 5

"I'm glad Mom isn't sick anymore. I know she's happy in heaven, but I really miss her."
— Lucas, age 7

Be at peace because God is taking care of your loved one. God wants to take care of you too, so He sent Jesus the Good Shepherd, who loves you. He leads you to quiet waters and green pastures by giving you all that you need—food, clothing, house, home, a family.

When we grieve, we might feel confused.

"I'm starting to forget what Grandma looks like. When that happens, I look at pictures. Lots of pictures.

— Mary, age 5

"I made a remembering album. It reminds me of all the good times we had together."
— Keosha, age 9

"People tell me Grandpa is in a better place, but I want him here with me."
— Johnny, age 5

Jesus, your Good Shepherd, cares for you.
He restores your soul and guides you in
paths of righteousness by speaking to you
through His Word, answering your prayers,
and preparing a place for you in heaven.

Sometimes we feel afraid after someone we love has died.

"Did I do something wrong? Is that why Grandpa won't come back?"
— Lily, age 4

"Sometimes I wonder if I'll ever not feel scared."
— Cathy, age 10

"I lie awake at night and wish Mommy were still here."
— Peter, age 6

———— ⸎ ————

Jesus, your Good Shepherd, cares for you. He walks with you through the valley of the shadow of death. He is your constant friend and companion.

———— ⸎ ————

Grief can also make us feel angry.

"Why did Grandma have to go away? It's not fair!" — Matthew, age 8

"I feel all alone. Why can't Mommy come back?" — Mia, age 5

Jesus, your Good Shepherd, cares for you.
He is with you through the days of grief
and sadness. With Jesus, you fear no evil.

We can use our ears, our voices, and our hands to help us get through our grief.

Pray.

"When I pray, I tell God how sad and lonely I am." — Brad, age 11

"I pray for my dad. He looks so sad all the time." — Susie, age 6

"I thank God for my Grandma. I really miss her, but I'm so glad she was part of my life."

— Kasey, age 9

Help.

"I can tell that Mom misses Grandma too. Whenever she cries, I give her a hug." — Simon, age 7

"I go over to Grandpa's house more, so he doesn't have to be alone."
—Melissa, age 12

Listen.

"Remembering that Jesus died for me makes me think He'll give me lots of other good things too."

— Lawrence, age 9

"Listening to the Bible helps me remember that God loves me."

— Lexie, age 6

Wait.

"I think it's getting easier every day. But I think I'll always miss Grandma."
— Gregory, age 9

"Some days I feel really sad, but other days, it's easier." —Maddie, age 6

"I know that God is taking care of Grandpa. That makes it easier."
— Sam, age 5

*And Jesus, your Good Shepherd, will
continue to care for you and be with you all
the days of your life. And you will dwell in
the house of the Lord forever.*